OPENING

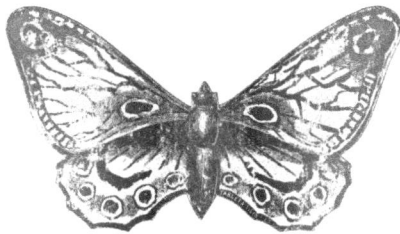

poems
Jean Lyford

Azalea Art Press
Berkeley . California

ISBN: 978-0-9908456-3-8

Other titles by Jean Lyford:

Remembrances
Waiting for the Wind
Waves of Time

CONTENTS

July 2014

August 2014

September 2014

October 2014

Coda

Foreword

As Jean Lyford's publisher and as her friend, I feel that I have been blessed beyond measure. Anyone who knew Jean would of course tell you the same thing—it is rare to have someone in your life with the kind of strength, integrity and positive life spirit that Jean exemplified. She was, and continues to be, an inspiration.

Jean was an educator and then a middle-school principal for most of her working life. Once she retired, she aspired to be a writer of fiction and memoir. Five years ago, however, she joined Hummingwords, a writing workshop taught by Cynthia Leslie-Bole in Orinda, California, and there Jean unexpectedly found her true passion. She began writing poem after poem, allowing herself to be swept away by the lyrical expression that flowed from her deepest self.

No matter when or why we are called to it, poetry demands that we pay attention to the world in an entirely different way. Jean quickly discovered that being a poet was not just a choice—it was a necessity and a destiny. She found herself newly invigorated by her love affair with words, and there was just no stopping her.

The poetry flowed without effort and without cease. She published one book and another, and then, when she was diagnosed with stage-four breast cancer, yet another book emerged offering poems that chronicled her remarkable journey.

Throughout it all, Jean was buoyed by the act of putting pen to paper, keeping her mind tuned to the truths unfolding inside her. Her writing group supported her through the inevitable suffering and the re-prieves cancer entails. The catharsis of weekly writing offered Jean a life raft, enabling her to continue evolving even as her body weakened.

In this, her fourth and last title, Jean contemplates completing her experience on the physical plane and gives us a glimpse of the transformation that awaits us all. Her poems are written from the perspective of one who has a foot in each world and is preparing to step fully into the next. Poignant, sad, and painful, but also full of joy and hope, Jean's poems mirror deep human truths while also being grounded in the marvel of temporal nature.

Jean left this world on December 8, 2014.

These poems are spiritual flowers that will forever blossom with the love and awareness that Jean poured in-to them. They are, and will always be, evocative of Jean's most beautiful, ethereal being.

—Karen Mireau
January 2015

OPENING

April

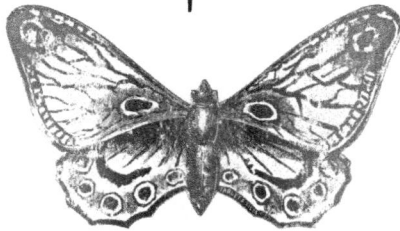

Drops of Time

dripping inexorably
never stopping
sometimes slowing
thickening
oozing
through fine filters
spreading slowly
collecting into bubbles

particles of existence
swelling
then popping
splaying
the leftovers
of time

Burn

burn burn burn
creeping
down my spine
swirling at hips
stretching to arms
then legs
warm
but not to touch
lingering
spreading
retreating for a time
waiting
gathering needles
to pierce anew

Dancing Leaves

myrtle leaves
swaying
catching the breeze
a languorous beat
hesitating
now and then
as if to take a breath
then
catching movement once more
a staccato song
of spring

new leaves
pale green
almost transparent
showing off tiny veins
that structure each leaf
clutching stem and branch
otherwise
they might dance off
lose their place in time
miss the brilliant blooms
of summer

Crocosmia

a mass of fiery crocosmia
guards the hillside
invites gasps of awe
deep orange beauty
on flowered stalks
leaning toward the sun
competing with light
burning toward it
demanding attention
calling out
remember me

Philadelphia

mock orange
weigela
and lilacs
mix loveliness with
the sad smells of spring
bring back memories
hop scotch
jump rope
then adolescent angst
but beautiful pain
like Byron's *patetique*
a love of
melancholy
philosophy
questions without answers
wondering
without questions
living on feeling's edge
carving awareness
digging
searching
before learning to accept
a new dream
less certain
finding a place
filling the yearning
until ambiguity
becomes a challenge

no longer a wound
but a willingness to see

the scents of home
carried eighty years
flood a new garden
in a new home
where new birds
sit on the *philadelphus*
singing a new song

MAY

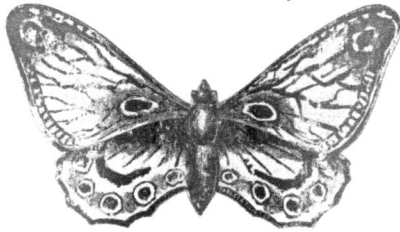

The Garden's Spring

the garden comes to meet me
full of leaves and light
full of life and hope
surrounding me
in an embrace
a promise of
buds and blossoms

wild flower volunteers
mix in the undergrowth
below foxglove spires
and rose bushes
pressing incipient
wine-colored leaves
preparing for blooms

forget-me-nots reappear
filling in spaces beneath
Japanese maples
waving their lacy arms
of bronze and lime

yellow-eyed daisies face the sun
sheltered by Mexican lavender
matched in height
by golden clumps
laddered on Jerusalem Sage

multi-colored bearded iris
pop up here and there
geraniums start first flowering
in slightly garish tones
next to peony's purple shoots
soon to be red or pink or even white

the garden
borrowed from the world
finding a place together
in a slightly tamed
but still wild Eden
where years have nourished
a gardener's essence

Loop

the glue that holds me together
has dried out
brittle now
flaking
pulling away from the core
small pieces
bits of the past
fly by
rewinding former days
only to replay
a loop of time
that no longer binds
nor builds upon itself
a paper doll life
with clothing tabs
and smiling faces
puffed sleeves
and sharp pleats
that redress memory

once quiet days
or active days
no matter
held together
melded smoothly
into a total self
no adhesive needed
but the past that races by

runs laps in a loop
that cannot change
pieces flutter
then drop crumbs
forming a fragile path
leading nowhere

The Blue Spruce

skirts sway
from side to side
blue-tipped ruffled tiers
await music and castanets
syncopated dancing feet
tap black shoes beneath
Andalusian dresses pulled high
clapping hands
join the moment

the frantic movement
and wailing sorrow
is left to the singer
clutch the rhythm
tap and clap
sway and hum
dissolve pain
into a new harmony

Emptiness

jars cry to be filled
and refilled
even black holes hunger
fill those empty jars
displace air
emptiness cannot abide
spaces hold us apart
even though
they keep beans discrete
and cookies from crumbling

do not walk by emptiness
serve its needs
open the lid
let mystery's aura escape
replace it with something to share
let others know
as they walk by
something is worth saving
shells or marbles
pasta or beans
nuts or candies
see what's there
out in the open
protected by glass
but within reach of all
unscrew the lid
enjoy

JUNE

Fatigue

not a state of mind
but a body
that will not move
dancing in one's head
making memory visits to museums
greeting visitors
a few at a time
shaky hands writing in code
teetering vowels
wobbly squares
for m's or d's
faces appearing
on the ceiling
bodiless
bearded
in dark sepia
famous poets
stopping by
silently
suspended in air
without expression
so I will know
they are not real

Opening

open to the universe
to being
abiding
as gates open wide
laugh at limits
even small corners
show edges in a blur
of daisy faces
become refreshed
in the nectar of dew
reflecting
swollen bubbles
transporting the universe
within each droplet

Walking Woods

sometimes trees walk
not like Birnam Woods
but another way
pushing through thick air
fluffing up leaves
that flutter back and forth
showing green above
to capture sunlight
while hiding
an underside of paler hue

sometimes woods pull back
shifting away from view
veiled in fog
guarding dew
waiting for the sun

sometimes there's no movement
in the woods
still, desiccated air
plants trees firmly
without wavy images
of walking trunks

sometimes at night
the trees surround
forming a bower
safe for sleep

quiet enough for dreams
when one can
play hide and seek
with wandering woods

July

Roses in the Ivy

on the marriage of grandnephew
Lewis Jones Thomas IV
to Kathleen M. Donovan

dark carnelian
climbing roses
peek out
from a nest
of evergreen ivy
meandering together
beyond the garden gate
forming a new path
up and down the hillside
through the seasons
wading through dew
or crunching dry leaves
dropping blossoms
piercing thorns
yellowing leaves
stiffening branches
taking turns
when seasons change

the embrace
of roses and ivy
survives
sustains
renews

Episodes

events occur
whether harsh or tender
just scenarios
for dreams
writing fiction
reordering memories
neutralizing dreaded possibilities
of what may come
we call them episodes
skits
unexpected experiences
stories to share
we make them safe
no longer fearsome
just amusing
little episodes
that can be laughed about
now that our tears have dried

The Hopeful Cat

waiting for the door to open
sitting in a long hall
half lit
on a wax-shined floor
shadowing her shape
until
she rolls over
exposing belly
with arms stretched out
enticing
whomever may go by
to let her pass
beyond the door
into a world of toys
games with moving parts
future friends
from another world
with whom she'll share her scent

On Mourning

odes are poetic mourning
for losses to come
or those stored in memory
in quiet moments
a flood carries
waves of melancholy
in active moments
feet press forward
slogging tired bodies
into temporary relief
ebbing pain's power
off to another shore

August

Good Paperwork

I have good paperwork
they tell me
not yet good news
a time will come
when paperwork
becomes reality
and if it doesn't
I had something
to look forward to
yes
paperwork survives

Another Day

awakens me
limbs move
testing muscles
contracting
gathering
pulling
body together
into one entity
attending to pain
checking time
what meds are due?
any nausea?
safe to swallow?
yes
this languorous life
lingers
managing itself
carrying me along

A Muggy Day

I can touch the air
feel its pressure
almost see its molecules
breath quickens
arms feel weighted
like the day
senses strengthen
even roses cannot hide
their scents are seen
particles of mist fill spaces
as hedges nestle
closer together
hydrangea blossoms swell
world weary comes to mind
on such a muggy day

What Next?

in threes they say
really?
does intensity count?
three whats?
broken vacuums
cars refusing to run
shattered china
any bad news
or just what cannot be endured?

it does matter
a stoic soul needs to know
before permitting
tears to flow or
complaints to bubble up
before dissolving
into the pain of regrets or
the pride of silence

can the self
survive more than
three events
or does the number
have no significance?
perhaps
only intensity
has claims

something one learns
to control
taking baby steps
to uncyst pain's power

Hollow Messages

I get it
hollow messages
anger's echo
a slammed door
email in caps
hurried notes in code
still intelligible
intentional disregard
repayment
for whatever
the wind has wrought
or the day has gifted
messages must be shared
indirectly
subtlety
sent
received
but deniable

I'm Waiting for the Verb

while parsing sentences in Latin
or in German.
Verbalize up front.
Let me know what's important
NOW
not later
after I've guessed
and might be wrong
or possibly even right.
It's of no consequence then.
Tell me tales, tall or not,
tales that
tickle my fancy
in a language I understand
and jokes that
double me over
into a roly poly pudding
melting on the floor.
Give me verbs up front
so I can play with them.

September

Where am I Going?

does it matter?
if so, for whom?
for what?
just wait
for the next step
to rise up
make itself known
when you don't know
what to do
nor what it is
nor what it means
be still and wait
it may have value
even be important
in the scheme of things
you may learn
what it's all about
but not just yet

Petals Drop

petals drop in twos and threes
weighty in their fall
pale lemon leftovers
from a dying rose
announcing the end
of summer

Rays

daily I fall in love
with sun rays
angling across the picture window
carrying motes of possibilities
giving life to light
bouncing about my bedroom
pointing out things
I never saw before
a corner triangle
darkening the wall
or a reflection
in the ceiling fan
as it swirls
attracting colors
from the garden
each blade telling
its own tale
blue images twice echoed
as the fan spins

sometimes birds peck
at the glass slider
they too see darkly
looking back into the past
or perhaps ahead
as they attack their own image
or petite explosions of light
dancing around the room

touching cheer here and there
with high kicks

kaleidoscopic shades emerge
mirrors try to keep them
as a way to invert
from giving images
to receiving them
in warmth and understanding

this is not a sick room
it is a birthplace
for light and living
for dreaming awake or asleep
for stirring imagination
suggesting stories
absorbing visions
energizing the soul

What I Really Want to Say

is when will this be over?
When will I not have to
manage my body so much
alternating nausea or dizziness
weakness and weariness?
When will this science experiment be done?
When will I join the universe
perhaps even get to see a black hole
that's millions of miles across
not inches like the scan view
of my primary tumor
gaping
waiting
to catch those little devils I'm feeding?

When will I take them away with me
into an unknown mystery?
It is not written that one can be
in the midst of our galaxy
beyond our Earth
or ride the space/time continuum
but
still I want to know

An Imagined Place

I imagined a place
that may or may not exist
a place where dreams
make sense
where thoughts
are paintings
in vibrant colors
that lead me
through another world

fragile leaves tickle my arms
as I go along a narrow path
shuffling over a flowered lane
careful not to damage marguerites
a green coziness
embraces me
as I stop now and then
to look up as well as down
to feel the air's pressure
to smell the dampness
to touch this petite forest
to accept its limitations
to rejoice in its upward reach
its lacy covering that
rearranges the sky

this imagined place
wants me to understand
leaves secrets in code
is willing to share
if I try hard enough to know
to accept ambiguity
while attempting
to decode experience

this magical place
merges life with hope
and encourages
memories
dreams
and even reality
to dance together

OCTOBER

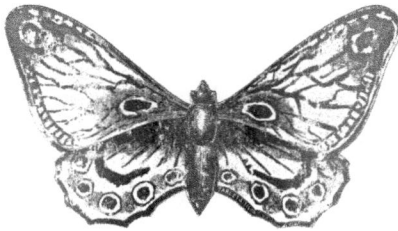

A Future For The Past

clinging to the past
keeping fear at bay
shortening the horizon
claiming ownership
like a child
who clutches a cookie
in each hand
hesitant to share
unable to let go
to find another treat

climb the ancient oak
a safe tree house
a platform for peace
savor the joy of being
away from doing
while watching the action below
and creating a future for the past

squirrels chase one another
overlooking my presence
but warning with chattering squeaks
as they leap and swing
almost monkey-like
from branch to branch
tree to tree
until finally

they scoot up the hillside
over the ground
that eventually holds us all
cloistered in the past

The Mask

let me go
cold sweat surrounds
with wet tongues
drops collect
run into eye brows
beneath the mask

release me
let cool wisps
cluster on cheeks
dry out beads
that linger
banish mist
swirling around
clouding eyes

when the mask goes
relief abounds
dizzy still
in memory
of a sweltering self
but no longer alone

Flee the Burn

flee the burn
though knots remain
pain's incisors
find the neck
fragile
lonely guardian
of one's core
master of the spine
the body's messenger
awakener
piping pain
stirring one's
awareness of being

I Will Die Tomorrow

I will die tomorrow
after birds awaken
and sing songs
when the air
carries sweetness
wisping across my face
a cool sachet
an olio of scents
claiming fall's
rustling leaves
and dry droppings
of golden, rust or red

there's still time
to touch mums and asters
to caress that last
full-blown rose
to inhale its perfume
holding one's breath deeply
until
the birds no longer sing

The Birds Have a Story to Tell

tap, tap
on the window by the feeder
black-capped chickadees
claim attention
tiny voices in tiny birds
but oh how they sing
flights of fancy
on tiny wings
sometimes grouchy
squawking at one another
sometimes aloof
ignoring every other creature
yet still on stage
eating as they test each perch
chasing other birds
forgetting to sing
but
I cannot understand them
their language is not mine
until one sings
alone
on a pine branch
with head held high
telling the world about
its desires
its dreams
sharing memories
in music's magic

Phase II

it's time to use time
to bid farewell to virgin hope
to greet phase II
with reality
as much as can be borne
now one needs
to get ready
truly
with enough dispatch
to mount lists
of the undone
to file recent memories
to recognize hands
that tremble
legs that bend
without intent
to let tears flow
unabashed
forming alien
rivulets
in creped cheeks
to look ahead

it's time to use time
that's left
mourn softly
quickly
then

write about
loss and meaning
love and being
holding self together
until it's time to say farewell

I Have Been Here Before

I have been here before
another time when deer
overlooked gardenias
redolent bushes
memorials
a prom night
dancing close
wrist corsages
wrapped around
shoulders or necks
full skirts billowing
while jitterbugging
another time

Dying Petals

dying petals stretch
a platform for bees
edges curl
containing dew
letting drops drizzle
slowly
cooling stems
taking away the burn

CODA

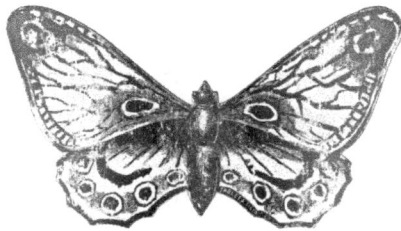

Wings

they weren't always there
wings
imagined at first
a possibility
but still a good idea
a node perhaps
yearning
to transform itself
from an elbow or a wrist
or an arm-like appendage
swelling to a distant sound
quivering
pressing outward
from an inner need
a volcano
still needing release
oozing energy
moving faster with each pulse
until a steady flow is strewn
beyond its nodal vent
a surprising power
first on one side
then the other
clapping
flapping
with the mere joy
of discovery

exercising
testing
training
its motion
into waves with substance
standing erect
dancing apart
while shaking
fluttering
in time to the beat
of energy's music

it is universal joy
watching others' nodes
swell too
being together in motion
flying
on new wings
that need feathers
colors
softness
and strength
to carry us beyond

Tributes to Jean Lyford

By Hummingwords Writers

Jean (Then)

Maureen Brown

She had already lived most of her life
But her story had yet to be told
When she arrived with her hearing aids and her oxygen
tank
And sat at the end of the couch
Insisting she didn't know what she was writing
As the magic poured out

The memory of plucking a turkey in Paris
The poetry of life in her garden
The mystery of outer space
The ponderings about the contents of her pockets
Or the box in the back of the closet

A beautiful mind finding the page
And filling it with wisdom
To hold in our hands
To rest in our hearts

Jean (Now)

Maureen Brown

Diving headfirst into a black hole
Anxious to have answers to questions
Not knowing what lies at the bottom
Or the edge
Or the other side

Just willing to travel to the pit
To the pitch
To the dark place

Our brave pioneer
Going first out of necessity
Out of curiosity
Out of control

And a joke here and there
To make us laugh
Or perhaps to put us at ease

She's tricky that way
Appearing so simple
So humble

Yet leading with the wisdom
The strength
The grace
Of the angels

Through the vortex
To everlasting light
And the love
That lies beyond

Jean

Ruth M. Grossman

Silvery of hair, wry of spirit, she sits comfortably in the corner of the cushy sofa, sagely looking out at the world, parsing her memories and wisdom for our benefit. A prompt is given, and half an hour later, Jean delights the group with tiny jewels of poetry. "Please send us a copy," we chime together.

Ezekiel J. Emanuel, a bioethicist and the older brother of the mayor of Chicago, wrote recently in **The Atlantic** that he wants to die when he reaches age 75. He believes that by then he will "have lived a complete life." Dr. Emanuel postulates that living too long in a "faltering and declining state" robs us of "creativity and ability to contribute to work, society, the world." He continues to state that by living too long "we are no longer remembered as vibrant and engaged."

I say, let him meet Jean.

Jean, who didn't discover her talent for poetry until after 75 was well in her rear-view mirror. Jean, who packed her life with service to the community, kept moving ahead, undauntedly, well into her eighties, inspiring her children, grandchildren, and her friends, new and old, with an open mind and an open heart.

And her family, colleagues, and friends responded in turn. Anyone who observed Jean reading her poetry at Orinda Books saw a women in her element, having the time of her life.

Cheerful in spite of infirmity and deeply appreciative of the natural world around her, Jean sets an example that 75 is not a destination, but merely a milepost in a life well lived.

I Took a Walk With You

Cindy Hoffman

I took a walk with you today, after the heavy rain,
along the Lafayette Moraga trail
I took note of living things as if your eyes were mine

A robin jumps back and forth
jitterbugging for food in the wet grass and leaves

A stellar jay, proud of its plumage
looks down at me as I pass

Hidden by graying brush
a flurry of tiny birds (your would know their name)
flitter up from the damp ground – so many!

A hummingbird perches at the tip top of a tree
a testament to the sun

To the side of the path in a gully
water gurgles and flirts around the rocks below, swirling
not quite enough to rush into a stream
but getting there

I hear the rick-rack of a frog and try to follow the sound
hidden somewhere in the grass close to my feet
he stops and I am stilled
when he takes up his song again
though I want to cheer
I close my eyes and listen
then quietly walk on

The grove of Redwoods whose branches only a week before
drooped toward the parched earth
wear a new do today curled and swept up towards the sky

Whipped cream thunder clouds rise
behind the green again hills
a flat iron freighter of a cloud
slowly pulls its heavy load low overhead

A few drops of rain fall
followed by a few more
and I turn back the way I came
walking the same but different trail
with a new perspective

A large tree bends over the path
broken branches, arching limbs
lean against a gnarled lichen spattered tree
I walk quickly under the creaking Widow Maker

There are shiny round brown fruits
the size of tennis balls, fallen from a tree
You would know what they are

Under the trees clusters of large creamy mushrooms
cap the mulching damp leaves
Which are toad stools? Which are mushrooms?
Do toads really sit on their cushions? Or does that only happen
on the other side of the looking glass?

You would know, Jean

Jean would know

Presence

Cindy Hoffman

Mulching together leaf and stone
petal and pain
bird song and soul
feathered flight and brittle bone

"Your turn, Jean"

"I don't know," you say, "it isn't very good"

a chorus of guffaws, "right, come on, Jean . . ."

You fumble for your reading glasses
or someone hands you theirs

and you read –

butterflies and flower petals
form from your lips
a towhee flutters in the air

Not a scratch of the pen or keystroke
what notes to take?
each word absorbed

and the chorus sings out:
'Read it again, yes, please, could you...'

And when you have read the last word

the chorus exhales awes and ohs and uhs
guttural grunts, remembering breath
from that heart place, touching the deep
the moist

most intimate soul

of this most intimate circle
of women with whom
you have written and read
shared and received from your corner
on the couch

where you sat on Wednesday afternoons
where your spirit holds its place
for you
still

Pardon our tears
as the singing bowl rings
at the end of class
reverberates in the air
as we speak our closing words

this circle of women
who one by one say your name
Jean, Jean, Jean . . .

Forces of Nature

Cynthia Leslie-Bole

I don't know how
to mourn
my dear friend Jean
I don't know where
the key is hidden

perhaps she
is the one best qualified
to teach me
how to grope my way
into realms
where fear and loss
walk hand in hand
with ecstatic knowing

when I conjure her
with my questions
she tells me to
erupt with volcanoes
surf with tsunamis and
tumble with avalanches
to learn
destruction and creation

she tells me to
enter the mystery
and feel nature
thrumming with
creative power
wordless wisdom and
limitless vitality
to find faith

she shows me how to
grieve and celebrate
as she streaks
across the bay
in slanted lines of rain
lit by sun
reaching through
thunderheads

she shows me how to
play with light and dark
as she dances
with midnight mists
over the face
of the full moon
creating circular rainbows
to underscore her point

she tells me to
apprentice myself to
nature's ceaseless cycles
to find the key
that will open
both sorrow and redemption

and so I will

following Jean
my luminous guide
who walks
a step ahead
on the path
that carries us home

Jean Lyford

Iona McAllastair

I would have loved to have Mrs. Lyford as my elementary school teacher. To have looked up from my desk as she bustled into the room radiating confidence, presence and interest in each one of us. To have raised my hand with a question, and seen her piercing brown eyes on me. I would have squirmed inwardly with her attention and with my self-consciousness before my peers. I know her response would have been a combination of clear no-nonsense explanation with a warm and loving holding, and then I would have known I had not been stupid to ask. My sensitive, reticent self would have been gently coaxed to show the class her love of learning and inquiring mind.

Today I sit in our writing group, in Jean's spot. I am at the right-hand end of the cozy light-brown three-seater couch, with an armrest under my elbow. A large sliding glass door looks onto the garden to my right, and Cynthia, our fearless leader, sits on her dining chair with her back to the glass door. Two fellow writers share the couch (whose middle spot is the least popular with no armrest,) two others share a couch along the left-hand wall, and two more are in upright chairs opposite me. We form a square of eight Hummingworders today, seated comfortably around our candle in its lilac egg-shaped holder on the coffee table.

Looking out at the garden in its wintry, bare-branched, soggy-leaved glory, I think of how Jean would have woven an exquisite poem from the images of yellow leaves carpeting the patio, the birdbath, and Ming her four-pawed beloved.

I remember Jean's presence the first day at Hummingwords, a lively elder with a mop of grey hair and sparkling eyes. Her upswept sentences had a humorous twist at the end, often self-deprecating. I remember how she introduced us to her oxygen machine, concerned that its clicking noise might be a distraction, gently explaining how it kept her alive.

I remember Jean's stories of her lives in New York and Paris, as well as her graceful allusions to the years of dealing with a husband whose mind was wracked with senility, and how she glossed over the trouble and trauma of it all as she spoke of him so lovingly.

I sit in Jean's spot and ponder a woman my mother's age, yet such a different character. A woman of many worlds, a woman deeply fulfilled. A woman teaching us by example how to face illness and change and loss of independence. Teaching how to shed skins like a snake. How to embrace death stalking through your body in the night, and nibbling at your bones, your structure of body-home. How to ride all the uncertainty that cancer brings. Metastases and radiation. Death with pain and suffering. How to hold the line of the battlefield. How to decide the limits within which the medics are allowed to wage war on your body.

I can almost hear Jean wondering, "How can I die like my plants? To wilt by drought or to be blighted by disease? How can the other plants shelter me? How can soil microbes support my roots, my stems?" I can hear her asking the Great Gardener to transplant her gently, softly, tenderly into her next soil, her next place.

Crocosmia

Karen Mireau

we burn toward the light
lean into the antumbra of the dying sun
falling stars from Madagascar
inflorescent, smelling of saffron
a common invasive to some
but ablaze on the hill,
outside your bedroom window
the last thing of beauty you may see
before the final shadow comes

the gardens you so tenderly built
for bird and bee and child will soon fade
their elegant, quilted plan will falter
the bulbs slow and wither
folding into the earth
as all things must naturally do

how can we begin to live with this—
the loss of you, your warm hand
your rapid-fire wit, the flowering of your oceanic eyes?
how can we admit how much you gave us
without knowing how insignificant
our own gift was in return?

we're not prepared for this
it's too soon, the winter blossoms not yet fallen
the croscomia refuse to be a memory
a scarlet grief on the darkening hill
they continue to bloom
and bloom

For Jean

Mari Tischenko

The macula may be degenerating
cochlea feeling only dim vibrations
alveoli weary, stretched and tired
and now, cancer
surreptitiously snaking its way into breast and bone

but she faces them down
for the dust and bother that they are
she has a grander picture
an orchestra
a mighty wind blowing at her back

nothing blocks her path
nothing silences the towhees, the fluttering finches
nothing blinds her eyes to the garden feasts of flowers
or the raucous symphony of nature
frolicking outside her bedroom window

for she has the gift of knowing
what matters
who matters
and she tosses it all to the stars with a grateful laugh
and strokes her beloved Siamese

who sits faithful vigil.

Jean

Mari Tischenko

we must bury our fathers
our mothers, sisters and brothers
and that family of friends
who fill the niches

the whispering cracks
where chill air wants to
seep through-
yes, those people too

she is Jean
she is light and laughter
strong in her weakness
bright in the dim of pain and suffering

she is big as the galaxies that catch her eyes
open her mind to endless wonder
endless gratitude
in a world of infinite possibility
she sees through clouds of fog
into a great beyond

she hears in the quiet of her deafening ears
the flutter of a towhee's wing
outside her window is poetry
on every branch and blade
hope and humor winding
through a garden path

her shaky steps are grounded
in welcome soil
fear, only a nuisance visitor
with a door quickly slammed in its face

Jean is, not was
she will always be
my muse, my teacher, my daredevil icon
of what is honest and good in life

her presence, her words
the flight of her thoughts
will cozy up beside me
with a warm cup of tea

and be my friend forever

About the Author

Jean Lyford was born and raised in suburban Philadelphia. After graduating college, she moved to New York City with her first husband, Gerald McKee.

While living in New York she met and married her second husband Joseph Lyford, with whom she had two children, Amy and Joseph, Jr.

The family moved to California in 1966 when her husband became Professor of Journalism at U.C. Berkeley. They settled in Orinda, California, where Jean pursued her own career as an educator.

Until her death in 2014, Jean lived in the same house where she raised her children, surrounded by her grandchildren Eve and Willa, and the garden that had been her constant source of poetic inspiration.

Contact

Karen Mireau
Publisher / Literary Midwife

Azalea Art Press
AzaleaArtPress@gmail.com
azaleaartpress.blogspot.com

Book Orders
www.lulu.com